Abraham's Blessing:

Ancient Promise And New Hope

....in you all the families of the earth shall be blessed.
Genesis 12.3c (New Revised Standard Version of the Bible)

Michael Caldwell

authorHOUSE®

AuthorHouse™
1663 Liberty Drive
Bloomington, IN 47403
www.authorhouse.com
Phone: 1-800-839-8640

First published by AuthorHouse   8/25/2009

ISBN: 978-1-4490-0391-3 (sc)

Printed in the United States of America
Bloomington, Indiana

This book is printed on acid-free paper.

Dedication

I dedicate this work to my children and grandchildren:

Marrisa, Alexander, Rowen, Pierson, Johanna, and Noah

And to the children of Earth, who all deserve the
inheritance of Abraham's blessing.

Acknowledgments

This project grew out of a sermon series at East Corinth Congregational Church, United Church of Christ. Hal Drury, Louise Sandberg, and Laura Waterman helped me transform the original monologues into book form.

Teachers and mentors who helped the editing include Bruce Duncan, Fred Berthold, Gabe Fackre, Winslow Myers, and John Morris.

I thank my daughter Johanna Caldwell for assisting me with Arabic.

Preface

The figure of the biblical Abraham looms large in the new quest to find common ground for the "people of the Book" – Jews, Christians, and Muslims.

These monologues bring Abraham to life in the present. They are intuitive impersonations of the Abraham character from the narrative in the biblical book of Genesis. They are fit for a brief sermon series on the life of the ancient patriarch who has been called "the first prophet."

The monologues could also work to catalyze interfaith activists interested in a dramatic way to enhance community understanding and cooperation on a local level.

They could also be simply read as commentary on the significance and power of Abraham's ongoing influence in synagogue, church, mosque, and in an increasingly diverse global society.

My basic question in looking in between the lines of the text to find possible contemporary words from Abraham is this: if he came back to life, what would he say to us now? What would he say in the "present tense" to ease tensions between members of his family – millennia after he lived and prophesied God's blessing for all families of the earth? Is the blessing still possible? How would he interpret

God's role now in the relations between people who trace themselves to him as their progenitor?

The project is offered as one new contribution to understanding and appreciating interfaith connections between ostensibly diverse traditions.

Table of Contents

INTRODUCTION

In the Spring of 2003 as I turned fifty years old and forces from my country invaded Iraq, birthplace of the biblical Abraham of Genesis, my children gave me a birthday gift that informs these monologues: Bruce Feiler's timely and compelling book <u>Abraham: A Journey to the Heart of Three Faiths.</u>

I grieved the onset of a new war and new suffering in a land wracked with violence over the millennia. I felt furious about the part that the growing imperialism of my country played in this new violence in the land of Abraham. I didn't excuse the brutality of the latest tyrant of this old land; neither did I excuse the false pretenses for pre-emptive invasion given by the Bush regime.

I saw hope in Feiler's book, because he makes a strong case that Middle Eastern misunderstanding and conflict might have a chance, eventually, to be corrected through the biblical Abraham. I saw hope because Feiler shows how the figure of Abraham embodies a historic universal link that could conceivably re-connect the peoples who are his spiritual descendants. Beyond the current provincial theological blindness of the "people of the Book" (Christians, Muslims, Jews), could there be a return to God's promise of "blessing for all families" (Genesis 12.3) through Abraham? Could people who trace their origins to the same source begin to see not only their common humanity but also their common status as siblings or at least step-siblings through him? Wouldn't that be urgent for current faithfulness to their One God? If "blessing" was what God intended through Abraham, how could recycled violence and war be justified?

After I read the book, it lay dormant on my shelf for almost four years. I felt immobilized by the magnitude of the practical steps that would be needed to bring Abraham back to present consciousness. But at the end of 2006 I kept getting flashbacks of Abraham's appearance in a psychodrama group in which I participated in the previous three years. There, I had surfaced my own anger by going into the inner life of the mythical Abraham, accessing his conceivable rage at the current misery in his old homeland and in the promised-land of the Holy Land where he had settled, seeing his children estranged there to such a great extent.

Around the same time, in a dream I saw myself bearded with a staff, bringing Abraham in character to the congregation I was serving as pastor in East Corinth, Vermont. That did it. I figured the least I could do was embody my hope in a series of character monologues as sermons in the new year. As Advent, 2006, began, I started growing a beard.

These six monologues are the written form of what I brought to the Corinth community on the Sundays of Epiphany, 2007 (which explains some of the illustrations). What amazed me as I leaped into six weeks of sermons without notes was what came out of Abraham's mouth. As I set aside the manuscript and started talking, Abraham took on a voice of his own. I found myself living intimately into the character in the preparation and the delivery.

I started with clarity about the one major theme which I reiterate at the beginning of each monologue: God's message to Abraham at the beginning of the the story in Genesis: "in you shall all families of Earth be blessed." I'd heard it before, of course, but it never stuck like it did as this took off. And out of that initial theme, profound as it was and is in every way, came three major themes that weave together the six monologues. They begin to paint the practical picture of what constitutes "blessing" for all families of Earth universally:

+the magnitude and portent of Abraham's universalist monotheism in the face of the provincial polytheism all around his clan's settling of the promised-land

+the stream of consciousness between the lines of the text that point to the archetypal connection between monotheism and monogamy

+the beginning of the end of human sacrifice

Beyond this, the first monologue outlines the meaning of "blessing," at least as far as I can understand it as a non-reader of Hebrew.

I am fully aware of the leap beyond the text of Genesis which the monologues take. What convinces me that they are worth sharing in wider circles is that the themes came not from me so much as from the character into which I lived and spoke. What came out of Abraham's mouth was much more from the Spirit than from my conscious intention. I couldn't ignore it.

In that vein, questions for the would-be reader: How did the Genesis narrative receive its canonical form? What editors pieced together the oral tradition into the scriptural form in which we now read it? What about the parts of the story that aren't written down? Are they any less sacred because they're not written down? Why couldn't there be great value in reading between the lines for the mystery of the unknown threads of the story?

I am not a biblical scholar nor am I an historian of the ancient Near East. What I bring to the text and its interpretation is a passion for Abraham's blessing. This blessing has potential for giving all spiritual descendants of the patriarch at least some common ground beyond tremendous and seemingly growing contempt. What would portraying the character who is the paternal ancestor of more than half the world's people bring to light? Would relating to the actual character beyond the scriptural page help us derive the peace that is implied in "blessing"?

In that sense, the monologues are much more expository than exegetical. And they modestly claim to tap into what Jung called "the collective unconscious" which revolves, still, around such a hopeful character as Abraham, if it could be but mined, like coarse ore still waiting for continued refining. The source of the monologues is in the vein of psychodramatic group process, as I have said, and in what Ira Progroff introduced years ago with the "Journal Method" – free writing from within the character. What would happen if other persons lived into the character, getting into his skin, and letting him speak, and watching what comes out of his mouth? Trying on these monologues for size may prompt more insight from a new Abrahamic community.

A WORD ABOUT
IMPERSONATION IN PREACHING

I also claim no expertise in character impersonation, or in acting. It is simply something I've tried over a quarter century of ministry in the United Church of Christ (Congregational) which has given life to my preaching. In amateur form over the years, I've given life to Moses, Isaiah, Micah, Naaman the Syrian, and Malachi in Hebrew scripture, and to Judas, Mary, Paul, Timothy, Philemon, and the figure of Jesus in Christian scripture. It is out of this experience of being "taken" by the character in the writing for preparation and in embodying the character on Sunday morning that I've come to believe in the power of impersonation for conveying all the blessing our our Abrahamic tradition.

Those who would try these monologues on for size should not look here for polished drama. What's here is a heart-felt monological rendering of what I sense the figure of Abraham would say to us, here, 4000 years after his earthly life. As a device, I attribute to him an awareness of the dangerous contemporary conflicts, theologically and politically. I attribute to him an awareness of the scripture of Jews, Christians, and Muslims. I attribute to him a self-reflectiveness that I believe comes with the mysticism of his prophetic awareness of the presence and power of God that I think we can derive from the record that we do have. If he seems to stretch the limits of what we imagine he might believe or say, may the reader take it with a grain of salt.

PRACTICALITIES

As I began writing the monologues, my hope was that they could be heard by all three of Abraham's primary families: Jewish, Muslim, and Christian. Shortly into the process I realized I could only really speak with integrity to the Christian congregation constituted by the people in the pews of East Corinth. It seemed presumptuous to think I could speak to people and traditions that I don't intimately know. And I felt my creative process somewhat stifled when I tried to speak to a broader group. I do hope that Jewish and Muslim readers might consider some aspects of the writing to be translatable, and maybe repeatable within the idiom of their particular tradition.

I begin each monologue with a Hebrew blessing and end it with an Arabic farewell as one way of inviting the inclusiveness of each tradition. If we're all children of Abraham, then he makes us worthy of respecting each other, and sharing each other's languages.

One blessing of writing for and speaking to the congregation of the East Corinth Congregational, United Church of Christ, is that it is extremely diverse. On any given Sunday morning, Christian people of every stripe from liberal to conservative, from former Catholics to former fundamentalists, could be sitting in the pews. In addition, many people who call themselves "seekers" (not ostensibly people of faith) could be present. I also shared a story each Sunday with the children and youth in the traditional "Children's Message" portion of the worship service, which kept me honest, and helped me keep it simple. To this intergenerational and generous congregation I give thanks for being "guinea pigs" for Abraham.

Some of the monologues are enhanced by short references to a map of the ancient Near East. I painted an imaginary picture of the Fertile Crescent with my hands, briefly with my back to the congregation, using my staff as a pointer. Others may find the use of a large map on display for each presentation to be even more helpful. If available, I suggest using a large scale map.

Throughout the presentations, I took the liberty of adapting the premier verse, Genesis 12.3c, as referring to "Earth" with a capital "E" instead of "the earth" with a small "e" as one way of accentuating our new awareness of Earth's sacredness and vulnerability. If we refer to nations without "the" in front of the name, then wouldn't we now want to begin to refer to our planetary home without "the" in front of its name? Could this be one small way to raise consciousness about the sacredness of the place we all call home regardless of our idiosyncratic cultural preferences?

I write in verse instead of prose, which lends itself to the spoken word better. It also helped me memorize the lines (not that I would duplicate them exactly in the spoken event).

I made a decision early in the process to use "Abraham" throughout even though God does not bestow the name change from "Abram" until Genesis 17 in the narrative. It seemed important to give a consistency to the character throughout, although other impersonators might make that shift a big part of the evolution of the character. Additional monologues await writing.

My hope is that the monologues might be a springboard for others to impersonate the character that gives us all new hope for a new diverse planetary culture which truly, eventually, embodies God's blessing for all families, bar none, brandishing "blessing" for all. May they be a source of new creativity and new direction about what Abraham might have said, and what he might say now.

Monologue 1: Ancestors

Genesis 11.27-32, 12.1-3

(Abraham enters with staff and robe, bristling with an awareness of God's power and presence, full of warmth, but also with a demeanor that challenges the listener. This is not business as usual...)

Barukh atah Adonai, Elohaynu melekh ha'olam
Blessed are You, Lord our God, King of the universe

Hello! I'm Abraham – Abraham of Genesis in the Bible, and of the Koran, and I greet you on behalf of our one God with one word for one Earth: the word of "blessing" for all families of Earth.

When our God said to me
"in you shall all the families of Earth be blessed," (Genesis 12.3)
God was saying something revolutionary.

I'm here today because, roughly four thousand years later,
the families of Earth have forgotten my faithfulness,
or they misunderstood, or the message has been corrupted.

I'm here to correct what's been corrupted in God's original intentions

and remind you what God's commission to me implies:

a world where <u>all</u> families are blessed, not just some.

I'm here because God sends me to renew the promise,

to encourage you to follow the promise now more than ever before,

because the consequences are dire if the call to blessing isn't followed.

I'm here to encourage you to continue to follow God's lead

toward the universal blessing God intends.

It wasn't an easy road to follow, then or now....   (REFER TO MAP)

We made it from Ur, my home in the southern part of what's now called Iraq,

up the valley of the Euphrates River to Haran in what is now Turkey

before my father Terah died.

It was a hard journey, walking all the way.

We had to linger in Haran to rest and get our bearings.

We still hadn't arrived in the land God would show us.

I felt "betwixt and between," and I was restless.

I missed my homeland but I knew we still hadn't yet found the promised land of blessing.

My family's situation was like a community grieving the loss of a factory;

Everybody's wondering not only about their next job,

but where the next meal for their children is coming from.

It was like your nation's grief in the death of an honest president – President Ford

It hurts, and prompts a longing for the old days when leaders had integrity.

There in Haran, we grieved the loss of our old life, but didn't know the way forward.

Your President Ford saw his pardon of Nixon

as a way of healing your country, but it cost him the next election

because the world's so hardened that it insists more on retribution than restitution.

It speaks to God's need now, as in my day, for a new world,

a new way, a new promise of blessing rather than cursing.

And do you really understand

what God meant by the "blessing" God promised through me?

When God promised "blessing" to all the families of Earth,

God was promising "well-being."

A word you might use is "prosperity,"

but blessing means so much more than material wealth;

it means security, well-being, and a sense of joy in life;

it's a condition that implies wellness for individual families

but at the same time, just as much, an attitude of fairness toward other families.

To be "blessed" implies spiritual abundance,

and a "bended knee" posture toward God.

Every year in January your president delivers "the state of the union" speech.

What would be the equivalent for "all the families of Earth"?

Who delivers the "state of the families of Earth" speech on an annual basis?

And what would be the content of that speech right now?

Friends, I can summarize it in sobering fashion:

the state of some of the families of Earth is good;

the state of most of the families of Earth is not good;

some say half the families of Earth live in poverty

or are afflicted by war, or are refugees,

or lack basics of shelter, food, and decent healthcare.

Twenty five thousand people die every day of preventable disease and malnutrition.

It is an abomination to the Lord of all,

the God of our ancestors who promised blessing through me.

Your ancestors – like me - expect a lot from you, as God does, in living into the promise.

We show you God; you are to show the next generation.

It's my father Terah and my mother who led me to lead you;

they both showed me one God -

which their ancestors from Adam to Noah

began gradually to see was the true character of the Divine -

beyond the typical ancient Near Eastern belief in many gods jockeying for status,

mirroring the idiosyncratic personalities and proclivities of each tribal leader.

Your ancestors since me continued to show you:

Our God is one, with one blessing for one Earth for all the families of Earth.

Different as we are as persons and cultures, we are all one in God's blessing -

when we trust in our God, and when we stay faithful.

And God leads us toward this blessing for all

beyond all our questions, doubts, and belligerence.

As I criss-cross your great nation, I find cynicism

about God's promise through the ancestors of eventual blessing for all in my name,

and I find it on both ends of the cultural, political, and theological spectrum.

Challenge it from both ends:

I hear "New Age" Liberals saying

it's only individual enlightenment that makes any difference. Tradition means little.

And I hear Conservatives, with their Social Darwinism,

touting the survival of the fittest as the highest goal

rather than God's promise of blessing for all, not just the fittest.

I remind you once more: God's call to me to the promised land

was a call to blessing for all families of Earth through me.

And even though it's extremely hard to trust,

God will open the way forward whenever it's unclear,

sometimes after a long time betwixt and between.

God does show me the way; you'll hear more next time.

God will show you, too, the way toward blessing.

Trust God, and God will lead you –

in your congregational life and in your personal and family life.

Our one God for one Earth has one word of blessing for all families of Earth.

Receive God's blessing! And pass it on....

Peace be with you. *Assalaam Aleikum.*

Monologue 2: Trust

Genesis 12.1-9

Barukh atah Adonai, Elohaynu melekh ha' olam
Blessed are you, Lord our God, King of the universe.

Hello, I'm Abraham – Abraham of Genesis in the Bible, and of the Koran.
I greet you in the name of our one God with one word for one Earth-
the word of "blessing" for all families of Earth.

I've returned after 4000 years to remind you of God's blessing to you and to all –
a magnanimous gift of "well-being" we need to intentionally accept.
And when we do, it changes our lives, giving our lives meaning, purpose, and energy.

This morning, I invite you to fully receive this blessing of our one God.
Receive it and receive inner peace, and a sense of well-being,
and be a part of God's intention that all families of Earth be blessed through me.

Reject it and deny yourself the spiritual wellbeing that transcends material things,
And delay the coming of God's promise of blessing for all, not just for some.

I was 75 years old when my father Terah died in Haran. (REFER TO MAP)
My family and flocks had walked hundreds of miles up the valley of the Euphrates

just to get as far as Haran, following our initial sense of God's call

to a new promised land of blessing. I hoped we had reached our new home.

We were exhausted. But it wasn't to be...

while I was still grieving my father's death, God called us on.

At first I resisted. It was hard enough to leave our original home in Ur, in Chaldea.

It was hard to trust. God seemed to be giving us the urge to settle,

yet we were kept moving. I began to understand that we were to head south,

toward Canaan, even though it was already settled, and the way would be hard.

How did I know, you ask? My answer is basic:

I prayed! But it may not be clear to you what I mean. Let me explain.

Prayer for us is as basic to life as breathing. In fact your English word for "breath"

is the same as your word for "Spirit," and "wind," too, for that matter – ruah.

Say it with me: ruah. Doesn't it ring with the feeling of the Spirit?!

If we pay attention to our breath, we're paying attention to Spirit; we're praying.

I open myself to God's Spirit every day through my breathing.

So if I'm out tending my sheep and goats and I'm breathing hard

(feeding and watering animals at 75 is hard work!), I just stop and give thanks,

because when I'm breathing hard, God is very close.

And I stop to rest and look to the clouds and often get a nudge from God

To pay attention... and God becomes very real when you pay attention,

through breathing, through prayer.

Every day is like that for me; over the years I've come to trust God entirely because God often gives me direction – maybe not right away – but eventually.

And even if times are lean, not enough to eat, and no immediate direction,

I still have peace inside; I know God will direct me if I keep paying attention.

And every night is full of God's Spirit too, so I pray to remember my dreams.

That's where I often get direction.

One night I had a big dream.

In the dream I saw all of us walking south from Haran to Canaan,

with green hills in the distance, and a sense of security, and a sense of purpose.

That was the dream – so simple – but I intuitively knew it was God's prompting.

I awoke refreshed and inspired, knowing we were now closer to the promised land.

I told Sarah right away – Sarah, my wife, my partner in life.

She began preparing food for the journey; she saw the light of God in my eyes.

What a blessing she is to me and to all of us.

She respects me enough to listen to how God leads me to lead us all.

That respect would help tremendously when we were faced with her barren-ness.

But I'm ahead of myself; that's next week's story....

We left as soon as we could take down the tents and pack up.

My nephew Lot was like a son to me. He trusted me as Sarah did,

and helped me convince the clan to move on again.

The first few days heading south went well, but soon we lacked water.

Our flocks provided meat and milk, but it took us longer because we had to go so far

out of the way for water. We had to keep praying for patience and trust....

I think of your own Martin Luther King, Jr.

God led him toward the promised-land of freedom and equality for all, not just some –

Part of the blessing God gave me to give that has still not been entirely perceived,

let alone received, accepted, and shared.

It was an ordeal for King and his people too.

Many died along the way, including King himself, killed by a crazy extremist.

But as my father didn't make it to the promised land either,

he got there, in a sense, through me, through his descendants, all one in God.

If we're on our way to the promised-land, we can die in peace along the way,

because, as the ancestors led, our descendants follow, trusting the way will be clear.

Think of Mary – the mother of Jesus in your tradition.

She says her blessing was from me! (Luke 1)

Do you respect Mary? Then respect me

by hearing my plea, and renewing the gift of blessing for all families.

And how about your personal life and your family life?

Where is God leading you? Do you trust God?

Are you in touch with God's intentions for your life and your family?

Do you follow God's leading in your decision-making? Is your prayer life real?

How can God help you go where you need to go even when the way's not clear?

We made it to Canaan eventually. I had a lot more gray hair by the time we got there.

We lost people, as did your Pilgrims at Plymouth Plantation.

As they feasted after tough times, we did too,

when I built altars at Shechem and Bethel, near what is now what you call Jerusalem.

It took a huge amount of trust and prayer, but we truly received God's blessing,

And hope it's received by others and passed along....

I ask you: Help me pass it on!

Peace be with you. *A ssalaam Aleikum.*

Monologue 3: Wives

Genesis 15.1-6, 16.1-16

Barukh atah Adonai Elohaynu melekh ha'olam
Blessed are you, Lord our God, king of the universe.

Hello, I'm Abraham – Abraham of Genesis in the Bible and the Koran.
I greet you in the name of our one God for one Earth with one word –
a word of <u>blessing</u> for all families of Earth.

I've returned after 4000 years to remind you of the blessing
and the "wellbeing" it implies, and to ask you to receive it and share it,
so that one day all families will truly be blessed.
Today I'm talking with you about my wives – yes, wives.

We finally made it to the promised-land
and we settled in Canaan after time in Egypt during a drought.
But there was still the issue of an heir to the promise.
What good is land without sons and daughters?
My wife Sarah and I wanted children, but we couldn't conceive.
As we grew older (I was 85 at this time; Sarah was a few years younger),
I grew more concerned. I was anxious, because God had said
"....in (me) will all families of Earth be blessed."

How was that to happen without children?

I found myself discouraged; God seemed distant.

But as if in answer to my anguish, outside one night, God showed me the stars,

and told me, "so shall your descendants be...."

and that my descendants would be "from my own issue" – my own biological offspring.

So I had hope again, but I did not understand how it could happen,

since Sarah appeared to be beyond the age of child-bearing.

I talked with Sarah about it, and she, knowing the importance of an heir,

asked me to take her slave-girl Hagar from Egypt as a wife,

and have a child through her.

It didn't sound as strange to me as it probably does to you.

There was a tradition of surrogate mothering in my time;

polygamy wasn't uncommon. Sarah's followed my lead so many times

through the twists and turns of our pilgrimage.

I listened to her; I thought this might be God's way of giving us offspring.... so I

agreed, wanting to follow her lead as she'd followed mine.

But then we went from confusion to complication;

Hagar became pregnant right away, and she treated Sarah with complete contempt.

Looking back, this moment was such a turning point for me. It was so hard.

And I began to think about the connection between monotheism and monogamy...

One God? One Spouse. The two go together.

Why? Because we're human; we're jealous and proud,

And those sins come out most transparently and detrimentally in the immediate family.

We need to minimize the intimate situations that can bring out the worst in us,

for the good of children, as well as to minimize the anxiety and tension between parents.

(Yes, it took time for monogamy to become normative.

Think of my grandson Jacob with his two wives and two concubines!

But the seed of monogamy was planted here, through me.)

Think about it this way, through a lens you can relate to from your generation:

in effect, Sarah is stepping into the role of the step-mother.

What's her role with the child Hagar will bear?

She claims it will be her child, but in effect, no,

especially the way Hagar feels about it, and she raises her child – a son – in my camp!

You can relate to that today because you see so many family situations

in your culture now where step-parenting complicates family dynamics.

And how do you think Sarah responded to Hagar's contempt?

She treated her badly, and then tried to blame me for the whole idea!

I told her "she's your maid; you deal with her" because I was at a loss how to handle it.

But it got worse and Hagar ends up running away.

It's here we get to one of the key moments in the whole story.

When Hagar runs away, God provides for her.

In fact, an angel of God talks her into coming back!

And the angel tells her to name her son "Ishmael" – "God hears" –

to remind her that God saved her from affliction.

Then God tells Hagar that even though he is Abraham's first-born son
and will not be the primary heir, he will be a desert-dweller
("wild ass of a man" isn't as perjorative as it sounds)
and therefore will live "at odds with his kin" because,
in living "on the edge," he will live close to God.

Hagar responds to God: "You are *El Roi*" ("God who sees")
because she knows she was seen by God
And that her son's lineage will be close to God, blessed by God,
even if not center stage to the immediate "Covenant" (more on that later).

There's something unique going on here, as you hear the story.
Although Genesis doesn't see my primary lineage through Hagar and Ishmael,
they are given status even though she is but a slave girl.
What's more – and it's not well known –
Hagar is the only woman in the Bible to receive the divine blessing of descendants.
In every other case, the divine blessing of descendants is given to a male patriarch.

So Hagar has status with God, and she comes back submitting to Sarah
because she has God's assurance that Ishmael
will be the progenitor of his own people,
"blessed" as "all families of earth are blessed" through me,
and because she has a theophany where she knows the reality and power

16

of our one God beyond the polytheistic gods of her Egyptian heritage.

Her conversion experience through the angel of God and her response to God
parallels no less than the conversion experience of Mary, the mother of your Jesus.

What you now know as Arab peoples are the descendants of Ishmael,
the son of Hagar and me.
Twenty-six hundred years later, the prophet Mohammed would claim Ishmael
as Islam's source of a heritage from me,
making Muslims part of my family, along with Jews and Christians.

People don't realize how big this is, and how important it is to recover.
Remember, "In me all families of Earth will be blessed."
Yes, and that means they need to live as family, respecting each other
no matter how different their lives are – desert-dweller or city sophisticate.
One God for whom? For all. One word of blessing for whom? For all.

It's why I'm here. Christians and Jews need to get with the program –
not my program, God's program – that all families of Earth be blessed through me,
meaning no longer living with the contempt that has characterized history,
like Sarah's and Hagar's "stuff" flung into history like a bad dream.

When Hagar came back, she glowed with the power of our one God,
For she knew she was a part of God's blessing even if life wouldn't be easy with Sarah.
We lived not without tension, but as well as we could,

until the next big moment God would bring – Sarah's son –

but that's the story for next week.

What I hope you learn from me today, more than anything else,

Is that both my wives and their sons are blessed by God

even though the Bible favors Sarah's lineage through the formal "Covenant."

So all my daughters and sons deserve the "wellbeing" God intends for them

through my blessing.

And what I hope you will take with you for your "discipleship" as you call it

is a fierce insistence on God's role in the lives of both my wives,

and therefore a passionate commitment to the harmonizing of relations

between all three of my immediate families – Judaism, Christianity, and Islam.

If we call Abraham father, that makes us all brothers and sisters,

or at least step-brothers and step-sisters.

And God knows that requires more respect, not less.

That is just the beginning, of course, when we learn to get along,

and put violence behind us.

For God's blessing through me is not only to them, but to all families of Earth –

far beyond the three religions of the Book.

A ssalaam Aleikum. Peace be with you.

Monologue 4: Sons

Genesis 17.1-8, 15-22; 21.1-14

Barukh atah Adonai Elohaynu melekh ha' olam
Blessed are You, Lord our God, King of the Universe

Hello, I'm Abraham – Abraham of Genesis in the Bible.
I greet you in the name of our one God for one Earth with one word –
a word of blessing for all families of Earth.

I've been calling myself Abraham all along but it wasn't until I was 99 years old
that God changed my name from Abram to Abraham. Why?
Name changes in the ancient world were about initiation to a new status of life.
God was initiating me into a new stage of life.... Yes, we lived longer back then.
Imagine it: a new lease on life at 99. But what for?
It was for the Covenant. Did you notice how many times the word "covenant"
comes up in the reading today?
In changing my name, God was making a covenant –
a contract between God and God's people
to inhabit the land of Canaan and be a source of blessing for all families.

It also meant I'd be a father for the second time,
and that Sarah – no longer Sarai but Sarah – would be a mother for the first time –

at age 90! Things were different back in our day, yes, but not that different.

This was truly miraculous, and it was through Sarah's birth of Isaac

that God would make the covenant – yes, with my second born, not my first born –

and I wasn't happy about it....

I'd argued with God before about the destruction of Sodom (see Genesis 18.23-33).

I argued again when God announced this new twist, initiating the covenant.

Why couldn't Ishmael be the bearer of the covenant? God only knows.

Long story short, God won the argument. Only one of my sons could be the bearer,

and it was to be the son of Sarah and me after all.

The birth went well – no complications – and Isaac was circumcised

when he was 8 days old; we were a people of circumcision now, since the Covenant.

Circumcision was the way that God established a connection, personally –

with all the men folk, at least; it was a patriarchal time.

It was a sign of membership in the Covenant community,

but it wasn't particular only to us.   Other tribes practiced circumcision too.

It was good hygiene when washing every day wasn't possible.

When Isaac was weaned at about 3, Sarah saw Ishmael playing with him –

a 16 year old playing with his 3 year old brother, harmlessly.

But something clicked for Sarah. The jealous mother could not stand

to see the 2 boys on the same level; she demanded Hagar and Ishmael be banished.

That set off one of the worst arguments we ever had.

Banish my son to the desert? How could they survive?

But God intervened again. I'd have to let Sarah have her way.

It had been so hard for so long already; it would only get worse between the two moms.

So I sent them off, with all the food and water they could carry,

knowing it wouldn't be enough, but reminding Hagar of God's promises to her

and to Ishmael that he too would be the father of many tribes,

having his own heritage and lineage.

That was the last time I ever saw my son Ishmael. I grieved deeply.

I poured myself into being the best father to Isaac that I could.

We were both tested by God on Mt. Moriah when he was coming of age.

But that's the story for next week...

When Sarah died I grieved again, and tried again to do my best for Isaac.

I worked hard to find him a wife – Rebekah –

from the old clan in Haran.

And when Isaac left to start a family of his own, I was by myself and lonely.

So I took another wife, Keturah, and had six more sons with her.

I died when I was 175 years old.

Who was to bury me in the plot I'd bought in Hebron?

Isaac, of course, but Ishmael was found and informed and came to the burial.

Together, as I understand it, they prayed prayers of thanksgiving for my life,

and for the blessing I'd brought from God to both of them and their descendants.

So here's my prayer for their descendants in Hebron,

where today there is warring and bloodshed and division of families:

Dear God, I pray they may all come again to my tomb in Hebron and pray together.

Are you not God for them together?

Can you not work a new miracle of birth and initiate a new covenant today

where the blessing you gave me – wellbeing for all families of Earth – truly comes?

I am not Jewish, Christian, or Muslim, yet all these descendants of mine

count themselves as my children.

If they respected me they would put down their weapons.

If they worshipped the God I worshipped, they would let go of the jealousies

and differences that are still with them through Sarah and Hagar.

If they could see the urgent need for the basics of life for all my children

and could see how pouring scarce resources into weapons of war

takes so much away from a decent education and a decent life for my children,

they'd mend their ways. Dear Lord, help them mend their ways. Amen.

I hope you will be a part of a new movement to come again to my grave –

so that the Isaacs and Ishmaels of today may again pray prayers together,

that my blessing may truly reach to all the families of Earth.

Assalaam Aleikum. Peace be with you.

Monologue 5: Sacrifice

Genesis 22.1-14

Barukh atah Adonai Eloheynu melekh ha' olam
Blessed are You, Lord our God, King of the Universe.

Hello, I'm Abraham – Abraham of Genesis in the Bible.
I greet you in the name of our one God for one Earth with one word –
The word of blessing – wellbeing – for all families of Earth.
God said to me in Genesis 12.3: *In you shall all families of Earth be blessed*.

I've come back to correct what's corrupt – primarily the corrupt blocking
of this blessing for all, and the unconscionable disrespect of me - and of God –
demonstrated by extremists of each of the three religions who claim me,
but don't honor the blessing that implies living in harmony, living in peace,
as sons and daughters of Abraham together.

Those who would commit violence to others in my family, to others who call me father,
are committing abominations before the Lord. They need to change their ways.
Extremist Fundamentalist Christians, Jews, Muslims all sin grievously
in the dissemination of their provincial ignorance and hatred.
Tell them to read Genesis 12.3; no ambiguity there. So much misunderstanding....

I've also come back to correct misunderstandings of the story

of the offering of my son Isaac on Mount Moriah.

Let's start with some questions: How do you hear God?

How do you perceive God's will for your life and your family?

Is your ability to clearly know what God wants for you

sometimes clouded by the culture that surrounds you?

Do you ever miss what God is really saying in your attempt to rush to an answer

in a difficult time – and then realize your mistake later?

That's what happened to me when my second son, Isaac, was coming of age.

Isaac was the same age as Ishmael when he was banished.

The grief of losing Ishmael came back to me as Isaac came of age.

I became confused. And I loved Isaac so much that I became obsessed about it

I fell into the illusion of the pagans around me – that God somehow wanted me

to offer what was most important to me in the whole world....

to sacrifice my son as a burnt offering, like sacrificing an animal! How?!

How could I have possibly thought that a God of "blessing" would want such a thing?

At that time, the kings of neighboring kingdoms <u>were</u> offering <u>their</u> children to their

gods in exchange for the favor of their gods!

I was vulnerable to the practice as I recycled my grief, and I got confused

About what God was saying to me....

Fortunately, I was open enough in a continuing way to listen for the voice of God

that I received God's rebuke for my mistake at a critical moment.

I was so relieved! And I knew clearly God was saying "no, do not harm the boy."

And I also knew right away my experience would have implications

for what you know as the Abrahamic Covenant (last week's story).

What I realized was: our one God is very different from the gods of Canaan,

in especially this way.

Never again would performing human sacrifice -

let alone child sacrifice – be a way to appease God, or gain God's favor,

or prove one's faithfulness.... never again. It was a sea change – in your parlance -

and a cultural paradigm shift on the same level as monotheism, monogamy,

and the confer-ence of God's blessing on all families, not just some.

Isaac saw my faithfulness too, thank God, beyond his trauma.

As all my children now see my faithfulness, tested and tried, Isaac saw it first.

That's why Isaac carries the Covenant,

even though Ishmael and Isaac both carry the blessing.

Isaac saw my trauma – my anguish, my agony – and forgave me.

He healed from his trauma; his healing healed me, and gave me a fresh start.

I tried my best to be faithful –

including the faithfulness to advocate from then on against child sacrifice! –

or child abuse or neglect of any kind. It informed our sense of mission

beyond ourselves. But that had been growing all along;

think of the way I argued with God to save Sodom.....

It was a kind of "evangelism." We advocated with the Canaanites

Against human sacrifice, but we had to upgrade our method.

We didn't like the killing of kids going on around us, and they resisted.

We got militant in our campaigns against the old culture of Canaan.

I'm not proud of how we treated the indigenous peoples of Canaan.

At the time I think we were doing the best we could for our time.

Violence was a part of the culture - sometimes, we thought, the only arbiter.

Isaac, too, realized with me that our one God would never again condone child

sacrifice, let alone require it. No! That's not the character of our God!

It's another reason God gave me the covenant: to show how God is different -

wholly different – from the capricious bloodthirsty divinities

of the pantheon of Canaanite religion.

It's why my family was favored over the families of polytheistic religion –

Because we offered an alternative to child sacrifice for one thing.

We became monotheistic as we became monogamous as we prohibited human sacrifice

All of that was a part of what could be called my "blessing" (Genesis 12.3)

that always included these three elements without fail.

We came to expect it,

but it complicated our relations with our Canaanite neighbors

because our ethics were so diametrically opposed.

We exhibited the first signs of the contentiousness of the Holy Land 4000 years

ago – contentiousness that continues to your day, and needs to stop.

So the story, ironically, is about the _end_ of child sacrifice!

And that, more than anything else, is why the story needs repeating!

Not to show my faithfulness to God, though; it was a misreading of God's will.

What God was actually doing was using me, my agonizing and my anguish

over the unthinkable act of killing a son (from deep unconscious origins)

to move Earth to a new ethic.

It would be a world where human sacrifice would have no part,

and any semblance of divine sanction for it would be roundly dismissed as blasphemy!

And there's something else here that is also misunderstood and needs correcting.

The text doesn't say the obvious:

Never again in scripture does God demand the offering of a son

except unless you believe the theology of some Christians

who think it was God who offered up his son on Calvary – (in your Christianity).

While respecting the people who promote this theology,

Their theology needs rebuke! The misunderstanding began with me.

Let's correct it:

A loving God demands no propitiary sacrifice to buy the favor of God!

That's true of animals as well as people!

God doesn't need our sacrifice of animals either!

The prophets denounced this idolatry 2600 - 2700 years ago.

A theology of sacrifice is not central to God's plans

for God's "kingdom on earth as it is in heaven."

What's central is blessing! – living out the ethic of blessing – wellbeing –

For all families of Earth, and actively working to make that happen.

That's not to say Christ didn't sacrifice himself,

or that you don't sacrifice your time and talent on his behalf.

But it's not about a father sacrificing a son to make things right.

No, that would always be a misconception.

It's the prophet Micah that echoes the shift most clearly.

His question: "What does God require of you?"

His answer: "Do justice, love kindness, and walk humbly with your God." (Micah 6.8)

That shift in understanding the character and expectations of God began with me,

Especially around the time of my experience with Isaac on Mount Moriah.

Well, I'm glad we've had this time together. I'll be back for the last time next week.

I know what I've said stretches your understanding. It's why I've returned.

It's urgent we correct what's corrupt, and receive God's blessing for all....

A ssalaam aleikum... Peace be with you.

Monologue 6: Hope

Genesis 25.7-26

Barukh atah Adonai Eloheynu melekh ha' olam
Blessed are you Lord God, King of the Universe.

Hello, I'm Abraham - Abraham of Genesis in the Bible, and the Koran.
I greet you in the name of our one God for one Earth with one word -
The word of blessing "for all families of Earth" (Genesis 12.3)

I've come to say goodbye today.
This is the last time I'll be speaking with you in this series of talks.
"Goodbye" in your language used to mean "God be with you."
That's how I mean it. More than anything else, I hope you'll keep our God close -
to you personally, and to your congregation.

For God's purpose of bringing blessing to all requires us to be close to God,
as we understand God, and to wrestle over and over with God's Spirit -
like my grandson Jacob wrestled with the angel of God -
for in the wrestling we'll stay connected in our common heritage of blessing
and in our common hope for the future coming of blessing, truly, "to all families..."
It wasn't always easy for me to stay close to God, as you've heard in my stories.
But I always felt destitute whenever I didn't keep prayer;

Remember the words of Paul of your tradition: "Pray ceaselessly."

The word we used to say goodbye in my day was a precursor to "shalom" & "salaam" -

the Hebrew and Arabic words, respectively, used today in various forms -

words with a common source, words that also mean peace, words that imply blessing,

words that both Isaac and Ishmael said at my funeral in Hebron.

I want to go back to Hebron again,

because it may be that in returning to my tomb, today,

all my children will find common ground again. Let's go there now.....

My tomb is in Hebron, south of Jerusalem, high in the hills of Judea.

There was something special that drew me to this place. In all my travels,

I kept coming back to this high country. I felt peace here; wanted to be buried here.

The locals - the Hittites (who'd also moved there from elsewhere) -

tried to give me the land; they respected me.

They felt the blessing of our one God through me.

They could see why God gave me the blessing to give, and received it themselves

and wanted to give back - in giving me the land which would be my final resting place.

I appreciated their generosity, but I insisted on buying it.

I wanted good relations between all the people - many of whom had come here

from afar, as I had, to find the promised land in beautiful Canaan.

It's too bad it takes dying to bring people together, but that's often true.

That Isaac and Ishmael prayed together to our one God at my funeral speaks volumes to me about what's needed in Hebron now –

where there's more tension between Muslims and Jews than almost anywhere else,

but also wherever there is conflict and contentiousness.

When I look back, I get the sense that God sees us thriving

through a healthy competitiveness. We can be pushed to be our best

by a good rival. Sibling rivalry that's healthy would be challenging, but not cut-throat.

It's a fine line and a tough balance, but that's what my Hebron tomb could represent.

If Ishmael and Isaac could forgive me – and there was a need for forgiveness –

and if they could see their rival families both blessed, there'd be hope

that in fact all families of earth could one day be blessed.

If you're tempted to believe there's no hope for peace, for blessing,

consider that if my life means anything, it's about my faithfulness to God

and God's promise of blessing to all families.

Knowing that this is God's promise took me through all my doubts,

all my questioning, and all my anguish.

If all of us have faith, we can cut through the old cut-throat ways

and we could have faith in God's promise of blessing; it would be the heart of faith –

beyond all human contentiousness, hatred, and resentment for past wrongs.

If Isaac and Ishmael can do it, all of us can do it. Find faith, find blessing.

Think of it this way:

In my day we made huge strides in all the ways I've talked about:

+faith in one God rather than many competitive provincial gods (monotheism)

+leaning toward monogamy after our experience of the jealosy endemic with polygamy

(my grandson Jacob's wives and concubines? A detour from the new route.)

+the end of human sacrifice, especially child sacrifice

+an awareness that God desires blessing for all families, not just some.

Yes, there was more to do; still is.

But look at the paradigm shifts made by people of faith since me,

who keep faith and keep discerning God's will for a new future, a better world:

+the abolition of slavery and the end of forced child labor

+women's rights and civil rights for all

regardless of ethnicity, disability, sexual orientation, or anything else

+the end of burning heretics at the stake or the hanging of alleged witches

+he practice of active nonviolence to settle conflicts (India, S. Africa, E. Europe)

+and the coming of more democratic political systems beyond the iron rule of tyrants.

What an amazing litany of change! – all of it through people of faith giving their lives

or a new future of blessing...

You're on your way to blessing

if you remember me, even as you say goodbye to me,

if, like me, you can leave behind what's familiar and comfortable

and follow God into the unknown, "whose dimensions may be known only to God

but whose mandate is to be a place where God's blessing is promised to all." (Feiler)

Remember me, as you remember all those who convey blessing and keep faith.

Think of what my namesake Abraham Lincoln did for your nation

in a time of extreme difficulty and courage.

Think of what the prophets have given their lives for in the face of great resistance.

Think of what your Christ did just before he died in blessing the cup and the bread

to be for you his ongoing real presence, making him alive beyond the grave.

Think of the hope; think of the promise; think of the blessing.....

Assalaam Aleikum. Peace be with you.

BIBLIOGRAPHY

Armstrong, Karen Islam: A Short History (New York: Modern Library / Random House, 2000)

Carter, Jimmy The Blood of Abraham: Insights into the Middle East (Little Rock: University of Arkansas Press, 2007)

Cleary, Thomas The Essential Koran: the Heart of Islam (New York: Harper-Collins, 1993)

Feiler, Bruce Abraham: A Journey to the Heart of Three Faiths (New York: Harper-Collins, 2002)

The Interpreter's Dictionary of the Bible, vol. 1, (Nashville, TN: Abingdon, 1962)

Jung, Carl Gustav The Archetypes and the Collective Unconscious (Princeton, NJ: Bollingen / Princeton University Press, 1969)

Levenson, Jon The Death and Resurrection of the Beloved Son: The Transformation of Child Sacrifice in Judaism and Christianity (New Haven: Yale University Press, 1993)

Progoff, Ira At a Journal Workshop (New York: Dialogue House Library, 1975)

An Interfaith Prayer for Peace

Lord of hope and compassion, friend of Abraham and Sarah,

Who called our ancestors in faith to a new future,

We remember before you the country of Iraq from which they were summoned:

Ancient land of the Middle East, realm of two rivers, birthplace... of civilization.

May we who name ourselves children of Abraham and Sarah call to mind

All the peoples of the Middle East who honor them as ancestors:

Those who guard and celebrate the Torah,

Those for whom the Word has walked on Earth and lived among us,

Those who follow their prophet, who listened for the Word in the desert

And shaped a community after what he heard.

Lord of reconciliation, God of the painful sacrifice uniting humankind,

We long for the day when you will provide for all nations of Earth

Your blessing of peace.

But now when strife and war are at hand, help us to see in each other

A family likeness, our inheritance from common parents.

Keep hatred from the threshold of our hearts

And preserve within us a generous spirit

Which recognizes in both foe and friend a common humanity.

This we ask in the name of the One who came to offer us

The costly gift of abundant life. Amen.

Alan and Clare Amos, Iona Community (adapted)